Rachel,

Best wishes on your special day, and may you have a blessed 1st Communion.

Love

Uncle Jeff + Auntie Franie

MY BOOK of BEDTIME PRAYERS

By Paul Wilkes

Illustrated by Sandra S. Shields

Augsburg

MINNEAPOLIS

For My Sons
Noah and Daniel Wilkes

MY BOOK OF BEDTIME PRAYERS

Text copyright © 1992 Paul Wilkes
Illustrations copyright © 1992 Sandra S. Shields

ISBN 0-8066-2592-9   LCCN 92-70386

Manufactured in U.S.A.   AF 9-2592

96   95   3   4   5   6   7   8   9   10

A Prayer about Night

Dear God, I know you love me so much.
Not everybody would thank you
for nighttime, but I do.
You see, I know why there's a night
for every day:
because I get tired,
and my toys get tired,
and the plants and animals get tired,
and even the sun gets tired.
So we all need to rest.
Nothing goes away at night.
Even though I can't see it,
my swing is still there,
and the trees on my street.
Even the street stays right where it is.
Nothing moves.
But nighttime lets everything
rest and sleep.
Night is quiet and it's dark,
but that's good.
That way I can rest.
And when I wake up, it's tomorrow already!

A *Prayer about Sunshine*

Dear God, I know you love me so much.
Sunshine feels like a warm smile.
I feel it
on the back of my neck,
on my face and arms.
The sun even comes
right through my clothes, so warm.
I can feel the sun
not only in summer,
but, *imagine*, even in the winter!
When the snow is so cold,
the sunshine is still warm.
I can't believe it!
What a wonderful gift you gave me, the sun.
But I think I know why.
The sun is like your face, I think.
You put this big yellow ball up in the sky,
always smiling,
to make me feel warm
every time
I see it.

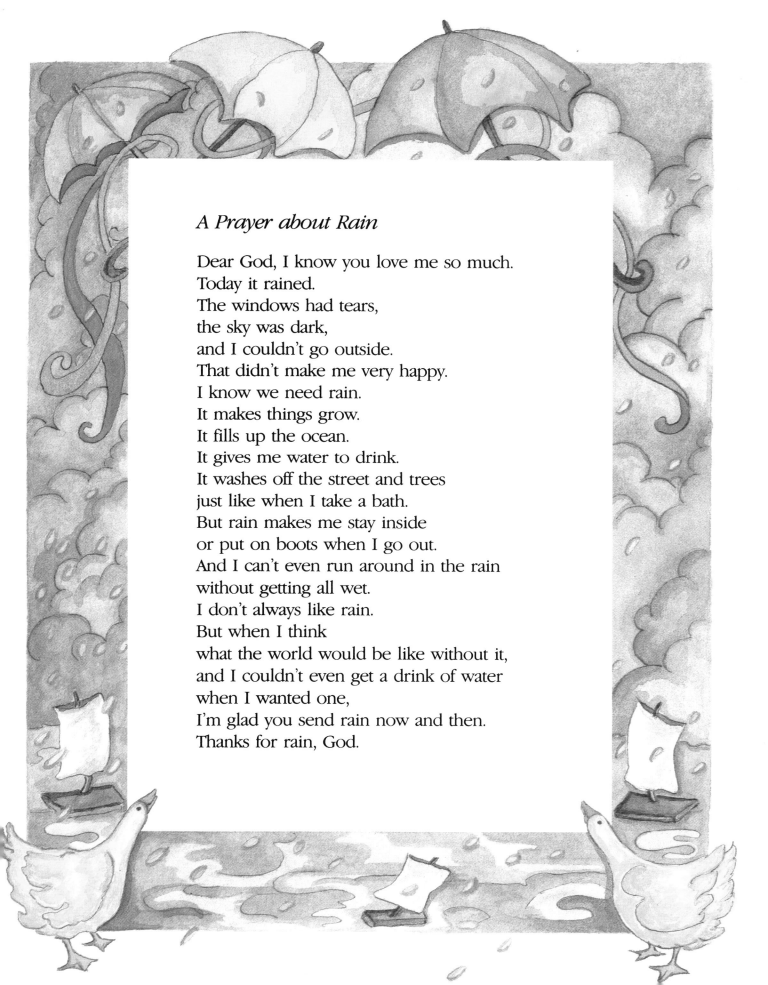

A Prayer about Rain

Dear God, I know you love me so much.
Today it rained.
The windows had tears,
the sky was dark,
and I couldn't go outside.
That didn't make me very happy.
I know we need rain.
It makes things grow.
It fills up the ocean.
It gives me water to drink.
It washes off the street and trees
just like when I take a bath.
But rain makes me stay inside
or put on boots when I go out.
And I can't even run around in the rain
without getting all wet.
I don't always like rain.
But when I think
what the world would be like without it,
and I couldn't even get a drink of water
when I wanted one,
I'm glad you send rain now and then.
Thanks for rain, God.

A *Prayer about the Wind*

Dear God, I know you love me so much.
You gave me such a wonderful friend,
the wind.
It does so many things
and has so many things to say.
The birds sail along
when the wind gets behind them.
The leaves jump up off the ground
and swirl around like they're dancing.
The wind blows the clouds along
and it makes my face cool
on a hot day.
I like to listen to the wind, too,
when it rattles my windows
and howls up in the trees.
And sometimes, when I'm really quiet
and lying in my bed,
it whispers really low
and only I can hear it.
Nobody else.
And you know what?
Sometimes I think I even hear your voice
when the wind blows.

A Prayer about the Moon and Stars

Dear God, I know you love me so much.
Even at night,
you give me lights
in the sky,
so that I know
you never forget me:
more stars that I can ever count—
tiny little specks
way up there in the dark,
sparkling and winking at me.
And the moon—
sometimes a thin, little sliver,
sometimes a big, round ball.
During the day
the sun is your big smile.
At night, each tiny star,
and the moon itself,
is a little smile.
I can look up at the night sky
anytime I want,
and get a million smiles
from you.

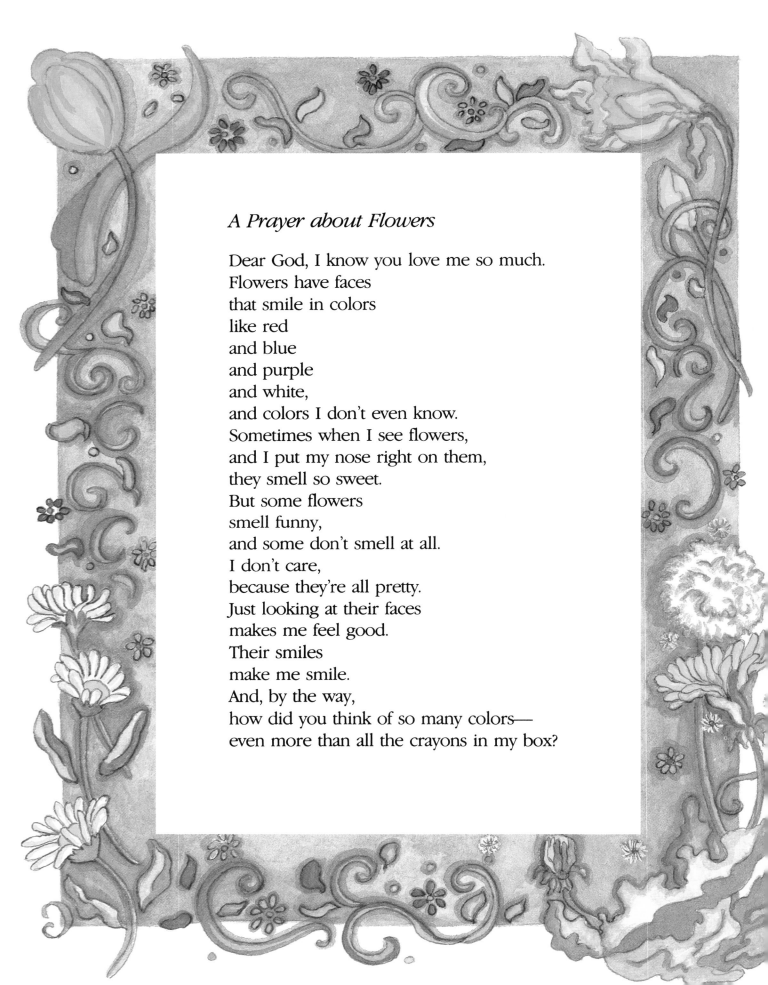

A Prayer about Flowers

Dear God, I know you love me so much.
Flowers have faces
that smile in colors
like red
and blue
and purple
and white,
and colors I don't even know.
Sometimes when I see flowers,
and I put my nose right on them,
they smell so sweet.
But some flowers
smell funny,
and some don't smell at all.
I don't care,
because they're all pretty.
Just looking at their faces
makes me feel good.
Their smiles
make me smile.
And, by the way,
how did you think of so many colors—
even more than all the crayons in my box?

A Prayer about Fruits and Vegetables

Dear God, I know you love me so much.
When I go to the store,
or walk in a garden,
I can't believe how many
different fruits and vegetables you thought of:
apples, grapes, bananas,
carrots, peas, corn, zucchini, potatoes.
And there are so many more,
each one so different.
Some are long and straight and orange
like a carrot,
or bumpy and yellow like an ear of corn,
or green and round like a pea.
Sometimes grapes are green and round,
but they're nothing like peas!
I don't like all your fruits and vegetables, God,
but I hope you don't mind.
Don't take any of them away,
because someday I'll probably like them all.
For right now, I have a favorite fruit
and a favorite vegetable.
So tonight I'd like especially to thank you
for my favorites.
Do you have favorites, too?

A *Prayer for Animals*

Dear God, I know you love me so much.
You gave the world so many kinds
of wonderful animals.
I can think of three special animals right now
that give me something every day.
First, cows who give milk
so I can have
milk for my cereal
and nice cool milk
to drink out of a glass.
Then, sheep whose hair is wool
that makes sweaters
to keep me warm.
And you gave
chickens who lay eggs
that taste good
when they're cooked in a pan.
So wherever they are tonight—
the cows whose milk I drank,
the sheep whose wool I wore,
the chickens whose eggs I ate—
give them a hug
and tell them thank you from me.

A *Prayer about Summer*

Dear God, I know you love me so much.
Thank you for the summertime
when everything is alive.
The flowers bloom,
the grass is green,
and the days are so long
the sun doesn't know
when it's supposed to go to sleep.
Bugs come out in the summer
and I can watch them crawl around—
black spiders and flies and tiny red ladybugs.
And when it's really hot
I can play in the pool
or get sprinkled with the garden hose
or sit under a tree where it's cool.
We go on vacation in the summer
and I have so much fun.
I guess
maybe I love summer best of all.

A Prayer about Fall

Dear God, I know you love me so much.
Thank you for fall,
when everything gets nice and cool,
and the leaves on the trees
turn whatever color they want:
yellow and red and orange.
I can march through the leaves,
crunch, crunch, crunch,
or jump in the big piles,
even softer than my bed.
In fall, the wind begins to blow
and I feel it like fingers
in my hair.
I wear sweaters
that make my arms
and chest
feel so warm.
There's a good smell
in the air,
like no other time of the year.
Maybe I love fall best of all.

A *Prayer about Winter*

Dear God, I know you love me so much.
Thank you for winter,
that time of year
when the earth takes a rest
and crawls under a blanket of snow.
When smoke curls out of the chimney
and long, pointed icicles
decorate our house.
Winter is when
I like to drink cocoa
to keep me warm,
and when it feels so good
to crawl under the soft blankets
on my bed.
In winter I can see my breath
when I play outside.
And when I'm inside
we make cookies
and I can paint pictures.
There are so many things
to do in winter.
Maybe I love winter best of all.

A *Prayer about Spring*

Dear God, I know you love me so much.
Thank you for springtime
when everything wakes up.
The birds sing again.
Squirrels scamper around.
And little blades of grass
push up to greet the sun
that shines warmer and warmer
every day.
I put away my heavy winter coat,
and I can run around outside.
On the bare trees
I see little leaves.
And in the branches
birds are building
their nests.
The ground is soft,
and it smells so good.
In springtime,
there's plenty of mud,
and you know what that means!
Maybe I love spring best of all.

A *Prayer about Mommy*

Dear God, I know you love me so much.
You gave me the best mommy
in the whole world.
She knows how to do everything.
She can tie shoes,
and button my shirts,
and cut pieces of meat,
and stack my blocks up so high
I can't even reach the top.
But that's not all.
She does other things that mean even more.
When I hurt myself,
she rubs and kisses the sore,
and it feels better right away.
When I feel bad,
she gives me hugs
and I forget why I was crying.
At night, she tucks me in
and gives me that last kiss,
the special one on my cheek.
Thank you, God, for Mommy.
I know she loves me very much—
just like you.

A *Prayer about Daddy*

Dear God, I know you love me so much.
You gave me the best daddy
in the whole world.
When I break a toy,
he fixes it.
When I can't reach something,
he lifts me up.
When we walk near a street,
he always holds my hand
so I won't get hurt.
He can do so many things.
But I like it best
when I just sit on his lap
and he reads me a story.
Or when he takes the pictures that I draw
and puts them right up on the wall—
so proud,
because they are the most beautiful pictures
he ever saw.
When he puts me to bed,
and tucks me in
with a special hug and a big kiss,
I know he loves me very much—
just like you.

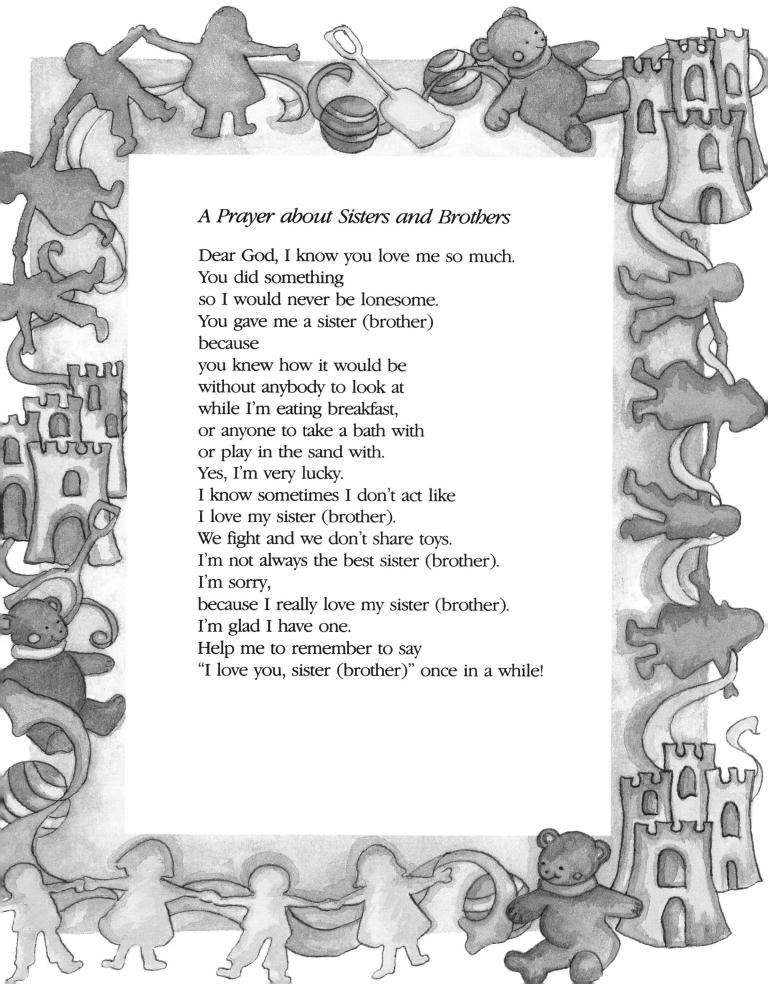

A Prayer about Sisters and Brothers

Dear God, I know you love me so much.
You did something
so I would never be lonesome.
You gave me a sister (brother)
because
you knew how it would be
without anybody to look at
while I'm eating breakfast,
or anyone to take a bath with
or play in the sand with.
Yes, I'm very lucky.
I know sometimes I don't act like
I love my sister (brother).
We fight and we don't share toys.
I'm not always the best sister (brother).
I'm sorry,
because I really love my sister (brother).
I'm glad I have one.
Help me to remember to say
"I love you, sister (brother)" once in a while!

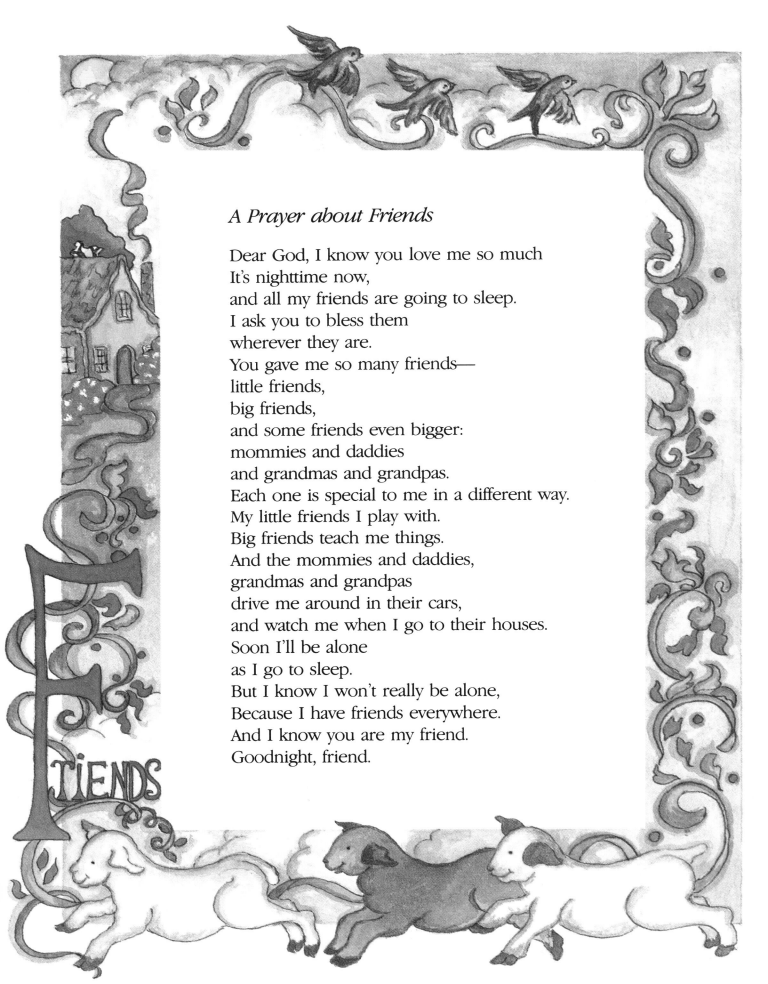

A Prayer about Friends

Dear God, I know you love me so much
It's nighttime now,
and all my friends are going to sleep.
I ask you to bless them
wherever they are.
You gave me so many friends—
little friends,
big friends,
and some friends even bigger:
mommies and daddies
and grandmas and grandpas.
Each one is special to me in a different way.
My little friends I play with.
Big friends teach me things.
And the mommies and daddies,
grandmas and grandpas
drive me around in their cars,
and watch me when I go to their houses.
Soon I'll be alone
as I go to sleep.
But I know I won't really be alone,
Because I have friends everywhere.
And I know you are my friend.
Goodnight, friend.

A Prayer about Being Afraid

Dear God, I know you love me so much.
Today I was afraid of something,
and I forgot
how much you love me,
and how you're always with me.
It's not much fun to be afraid.
I felt so alone,
like nobody understood
why I was scared.
But you understand, God,
I know you do.
Because you were right there today
And you saw and heard everything.
If only I had remembered
I wasn't alone,
and that you love me so much.
You don't want me to be afraid.
Help me to remember next time, please.

A Prayer after a Happy Day

Dear God, I know you love me so much.
What a wonderful time I had today.
Everything seemed to go just right.
It was easy to be nice
to my friends,
to share toys, to wait my turn.
It was easy to finish
the good food on my plate.
It was easy to do what
Mommy and Daddy told me.
I was happy all day.
I didn't have a mirror with me,
but I bet I had a smile on my face
almost every minute.
Maybe it's because you
were with me in a special way today.
And when I know you're around,
my special friend,
I know I don't have anything to worry about.
Thank you, God,
for such a happy day.
Please be with me tomorrow.

A *Prayer after a Sad Day*

Dear God, I know you love me so much.
Something happened today
that made me very sad.
I would rather be happy than sad,
but I know that sometimes
sad things happen.
I don't like it
when a friend moves away,
or when somebody who promised
to come and play can't come.
But I know that when something sad happens,
you're right there with me,
holding my hand and being my friend.
I can't see you,
but I know you're there.
And I know that soon
you'll make something wonderful happen—
a surprise, a treat—
to make me smile again.

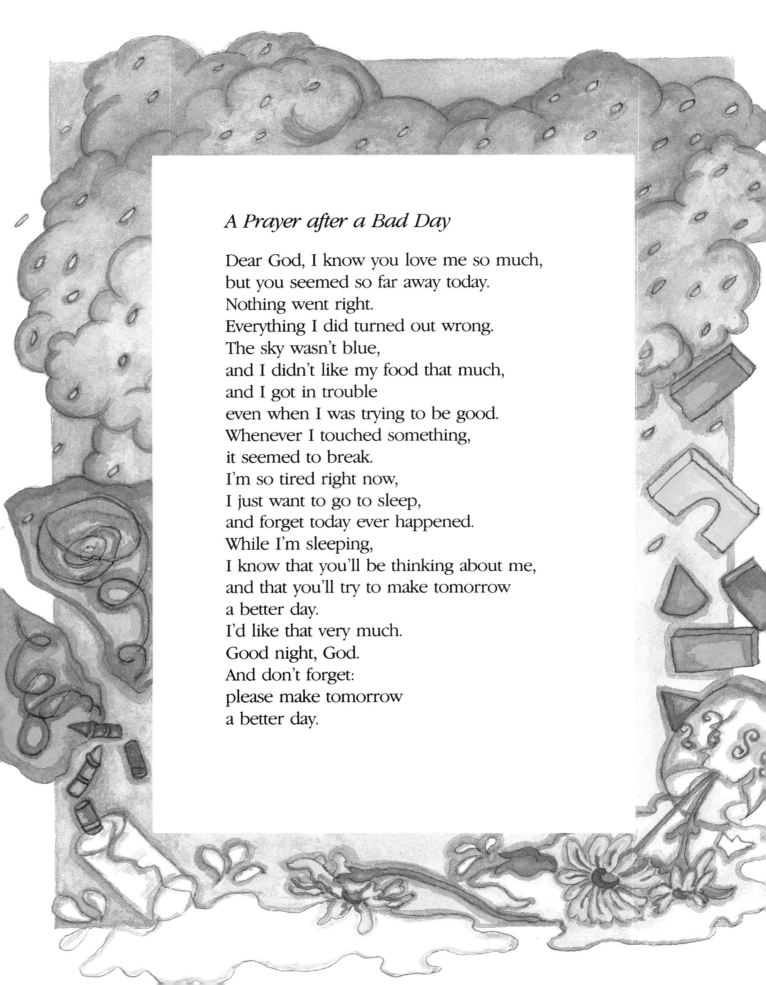

A Prayer after a Bad Day

Dear God, I know you love me so much,
but you seemed so far away today.
Nothing went right.
Everything I did turned out wrong.
The sky wasn't blue,
and I didn't like my food that much,
and I got in trouble
even when I was trying to be good.
Whenever I touched something,
it seemed to break.
I'm so tired right now,
I just want to go to sleep,
and forget today ever happened.
While I'm sleeping,
I know that you'll be thinking about me,
and that you'll try to make tomorrow
a better day.
I'd like that very much.
Good night, God.
And don't forget:
please make tomorrow
a better day.

A Prayer after a Sick Day

Dear God, I know you love me so much.
I felt really sick today.
My head hurt, my stomach hurt,
even my teeth hurt.
I didn't want
to get out of bed,
or eat anything at all.
But I know
that when I'm sick,
you love me even more.
And when I'm sick
you never,
not once,
leave my room.
You're right here,
helping to make me better.
Stay by my bed
through the night.
And when the sun comes up tomorrow,
please help me feel better.

A *Prayer for a Birthday*

Dear God, I know you love me so much.
Today was my birthday,
the special day you
made just for me.
Birthdays are wonderful
because of parties and presents,
cake and ice cream.
But I know birthdays are even more important,
because birthdays celebrate
the very first day I was here.
I was so small and you took care of me
when I was a tiny baby.
Now look at me, bigger and bigger
every year.
And I know that with every birthday
you love me more and more.
But I guess you have to.
There's more of me to love.

Prayer about a Visit

Dear God, I know you love me so much.
I'm happy
when people come to visit our house:
grandmas, grandpas, cousins, and friends.
It's fun
to sit at the table,
and hear
about places I've never been
and about doing things
I've never done.
Having a visitor is like
going on a trip
or doing something brand-new.
Tonight, I'm especially happy
because tomorrow
we'll have a special visitor.
I ask you tonight
to watch over our visitors
wherever they may be.
And bring them safely
to our house
as soon as you can.

A *Prayer before a Big Day*

Dear God, I know you love me so much.
Tomorrow will be
so exciting I can hardly wait.
I'm going to do something
I've never done before,
but I can just imagine what it will be like.
Right now,
I'm going to rest,
so that I can be
wide awake tomorrow,
so I can enjoy every minute.
You love me so much
that you give me
many wonderful things to do.
And best of all,
you'll be there with me tomorrow,
and you'll see everything
I do.
And we can talk about it
tomorrow night.

A Prayer about Vacation

Dear God, I know you love me so much.
Vacation is that special time
of the year,
when our whole family
goes someplace
or just stays home to have fun.
I learn new things,
and see new places,
and meet new friends
on vacation.
This year
our vacation will be the best one ever.
Thank you for giving our family
a time when we don't have to do
the same old things
every day.
Thanks for vacation,
when our whole family only has one job,
and that's to have a good time.

A *Prayer about Going to School*

Dear God, I know you love me so much.
At school
I learn so many things,
like how to paint,
and make letters and numbers,
and how things work,
and how to get along
with my friends.
I know you want me
to go to school
so that,
as I get bigger and bigger,
I'll learn to write my name
and all sorts of words,
and someday
even read a whole book,
just like this one.
I know that
school is good for me.
Like food makes my body strong,
going to school makes my mind
get stronger, too.

A Prayer about Doing Something New

Dear God, I know you love me so much.
You bring many wonderful things
into my life,
like today
when I tried something new.
It was the very first time
and I was really excited.
I guess I must be getting big;
I'm not a baby anymore
if I can do so many things.
The world you made
is full of wonderful things.
It seems that every day
I do something new,
or see something
I never saw before.
Thank you for all
the surprises and good things
that happen to me every day.

A Prayer Thanking God for Being God

Dear God, I know you love me so much.
Night after night
I thank you in my prayers
for the wonderful things of this earth,
like flowers and sunshine and animals;
for people, like my mommy and daddy,
grandpas and grandmas, aunts, uncles, friends,
and the visitors who come to our house.
But tonight I want to thank you
for just one very important thing:
You.
You made everything I see.
You made all the good times I have.
You even made me.
You are so good to me,
being right here with me
when I have good days
and when I have bad days.
Thank you very much
for being such a wonderful friend.
Before I go to sleep tonight,
I want you to know:
Dear God, I know you love me so much,
and I love you so much, too.

Author's Note

I began reading bedtime stories to my son Noah when he was about two years old. It wasn't long before I realized I wanted something more to offer him in those precious last minutes of the day. I pray each night and I wanted for him that same opportunity: to be able to place before God his thoughts, his needs, his triumphs and frustrations at the close of the day.

And so I went to a number of bookstores, both secular and religious, and began to buy books of prayers for children. But as the collection grew, so did a certain frustration. There were many wonderful prayers in those books, but I sensed a need for still other prayers, prayers that would allow Noah a more personal and comfortable relationship with God. Where I would find them, I didn't know, but one night Noah solved my dilemma.

Noah had developed a habit of mouthing either what he remembered were the first words of books we had read, or what the pictures or his mood suggested that they might be. And on that night, as I was pulling out the latest prayer book, I hesitated. In that moment of hesitation, Noah's little voice was heard.

"Dear God," he began. "I know you love me so much. I . . ." and his voice trailed off.

Where had those wonderfully intimate and reassuring words come from? Had I used them? For an instant I was stymied. What was on his mind? What more did he want to say to this loving God? I looked down at his face, upturned toward me, smiling in anticipation. His face was radiant. Radiant as. . . . I began to compose a spontaneous prayer, perhaps sounding more confident than I really was that I could actually do it. By the end of my prayer about the radiance of sunshine—the first I composed at his bedside—Noah's smile had turned into a comfortably, sleepy look. He snuggled deeper into his pillow. "Goodnight, Daddy," he said. "Goodnight, God." And he was asleep.

Nothing is more important to children than their own experiences. They live in a world where they are constantly monitored, told to do this or avoid that. There is a world of grown-up people around them, doing grown-up things—and children, who have experiences every bit as real and exciting and important to them as are our own, often don't have the chance to present and mull over these events and observations of their young lives. But, if they are given the opportunity to present to God what they have seen and felt, it shows them that simple, direct communication with God—prayer in its purest form—is as natural as talking to a good friend.

And so, in the evenings that followed, as Noah was ready for sleep I would try to think of what was happening in his life. With little more in mind than a snow-fall, a bout of the flu, an upcoming visit from Grandma Jane, or something that had frightened my son that day, I would bravely begin with Noah's own words, "Dear God, I know you love me so much."

After we had been praying together for some time to this God who loved Noah so much, I began to write down the prayers, remembering as best I could what had come from our mouths—for Noah often added his own thoughts to mine. As you read these prayers aloud, please make them your child's own. Personalize them. Whatever has made your child sad or happy, whatever fruit or vegetable or visitor is your child's favorite, include that in the prayer. Night prayer is a wonderful, restful time for you and your child to talk with God about the people, things, events, and emotions of the day just passing or that the day that lies ahead may bring.

Paul Wilkes
Hardwick, Massachusetts